Outliars

A Discourse Guide to Fact-Checking & Click-Baiting

Angie Waller

UNKNOWN UNKNOWNS

Outliars—not outliers. In statistics, outliers are observations that "lie outside" the expected values in a range of data. In a series of numbers such as 3, 23, 34, 28, 26, 88—3 and 88 would be outliers because they fall outside the pattern set by the rest of the series. They are much larger or smaller than the other values in the range.

Liar, a term not needing technical explanation, is someone who lies—a deceiver, a fibber, a falsifier, a teller of untruths.

In the lead-up to the 2020 election, my social media feed was filled with politely worded headlines covering Trump's bogus election fraud claims. I felt physically jarred when scanning these headlines with euphemisms for lies—phrases like *"false statements"* and *"claims without evidence."* The sheer quantity of these hedgy headlines only reinforced the numbness I already felt after being stuck at home in front of my computer during the pandemic, anticipating the doom that would result no matter what the election outcome.

Although the name "Trump" appears often on these pages, this book does not attempt to analyze his presidency or fact check his administration's claims. Instead, this book considers how headlines of the Trump era negotiated the fact of lying. It takes as its data set a 28-year archive of headlines* from *The New York Times*, arguably the most popular coverage of U.S. politics in the last four years.

Section 1 looks at how the transition from print to digital has influenced the quantity and types of content that are published in *The New York Times*. This includes a tabulation of Trump coverage compared to past presidents—dating back to Bill Clinton when the *Times's* website was first introduced.

Section 2 applies linguistic research in belief statements and hedging to lay out the ways headlines express editorial uncertainty.

Section 3 applies discourse analysis to parse the types of lies that are written about in the *Times's* coverage. Keyword analysis of these categories of deception reveals that framings such as eliding evidence, expressing certainty, and posing questions are recurring patterns no matter the severity of the subject.

The data used in this book were retrieved from the New York Times API—a tool that makes their archives accessible as spreadsheets and structured data for analysis. The critiques in this book are not constrained to *The New York Times*. This analysis can be applied to other online news outlets competing for attention in the crowded "breaking news" media space.

*All headline examples on the following pages are copied directly from *The New York Times*. Capitalization styling and punctuation from the original source are preserved.

Part 1.

Part 2.

Part 3.

Part 4.

Part 1.

Digital News

This section considers how *The New York Times's* headlines have changed since transitioning to the web.

When publishing online, news outlets compete for attention on readers' social media feeds. Stories are published at a more rapid pace in order to solidify market dominance.

When news was confined to print, headlines were constrained by physical space and words were chosen to fit into a few square inches allotted in a layout. In the era of online news, headlines are composed for search engines, where keywords and click-ability are considered alongside the story's topic (Christin, 2020).

Market Dominance

On January 22, 1996, *The New York Times* launched its website. By 2020, they reported having over five million digital subscribers, surpassing their print subscriber base (The New York Times Company, 2020). The rate of the *Times's* headlines has increased in this shift to the web.

Figure 1 shows the steady climb in the quantity of headlines published each year that included the sitting president's last name; transition months between election and inauguration are left out. For instance, only headlines with "Bush" are counted for the year 2001.

Opinion and Editorial headlines during the Trump presidency far outpaced this trend. Figure 2 shows there were **over three times** as many Opinion and Editorial headlines featuring "Trump" (n=911) as a keyword during his one term compared to headlines with "Obama" (n=256) during the entirety of his two terms. These "Trump" headlines were published at **more than twelve times** the average rate (avg. 228/year) of Opinion and Editorial headlines containing the keywords "Bush" and "Clinton" during their presidencies (avg. 19/year).

→ Market Dominance

Figure 1

News stories (non-opinion) per year

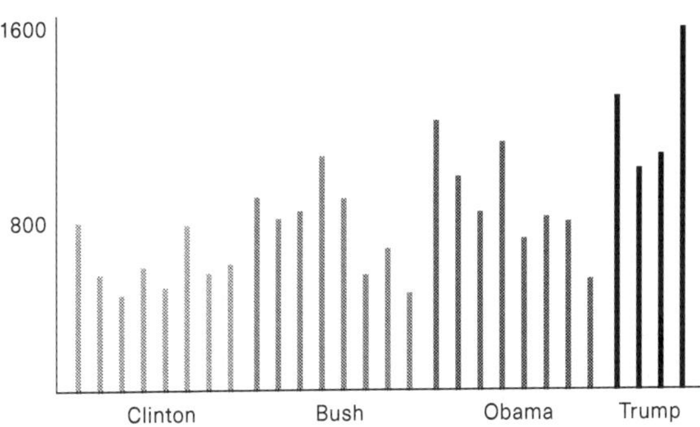

Figure 2

Opinion and Editorial articles per year

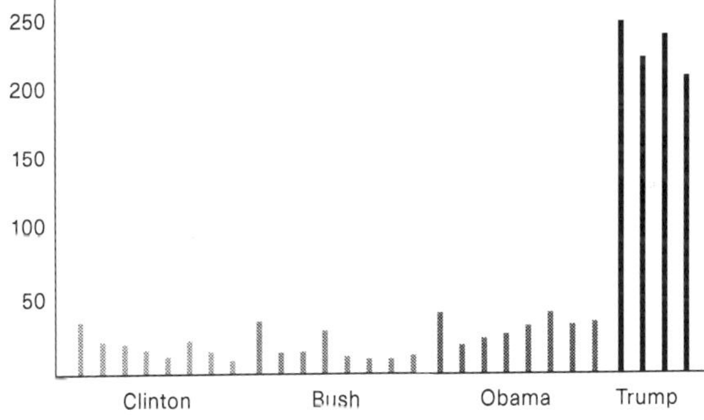

Counting Clicks

Multiple news organizations now use A/B testing to decide on an article's final headline (Jiang, 2019). These tests are run by presenting different headlines for the same article to different groups of readers. While these multiple versions are online, editors collect click data. The headline with the most reader clicks becomes the final headline.

These tests last about an hour, and only one story's headline is tested at a time. Experiments at *The New York Times* have shown that "powerful words" and a "conversational tone" can increase readership of an article by over 1000% (Bulik, 2016).

Headline A

$2 Billion Worth of Free Media for Trump

Headline B

Measuring Trump's Media Dominance

Headline A got nearly three times as many clicks as Headline B, so it became the final headline (Bulik, 2016).

Being Found

News outlets like *The New York Times* are competing in the same digital space as blogs, online magazines, and social media content. To rise above the crowd in Google search results, they deliberately use search engine optimization (SEO). SEO strategies utilize more keywords based on trending topics, and specific word order for search crawlers. Even the use of punctuation has been found to make a difference in discoverability (Christin, 2020). Headline writers trained in SEO techniques experiment with these formulas to increase the likelihood that a link to their story will appear at the top of search engine results (Christin, 2020).

Focusing on *The New York Times* headlines that included the sitting president's last name, Figure 3 shows how the number of words per headline has steadily increased since 1993.

Figure 4 shows a dramatic climb in the use of "?" in Trump headlines, with a rate of **over four times** (avg. of 175/year) that of Obama headlines (avg. of 39/year) during each of their terms. This choice of punctuation has implications for the ways that lies are called out. Journalist's point of view through posing questions is considered in more detail on p. 24.

Figure 3

Average word count per headline per year

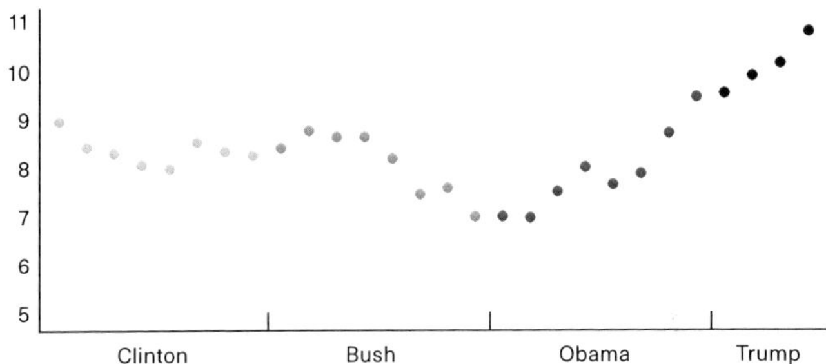

Figure 4

Count of headlines with "?" per year

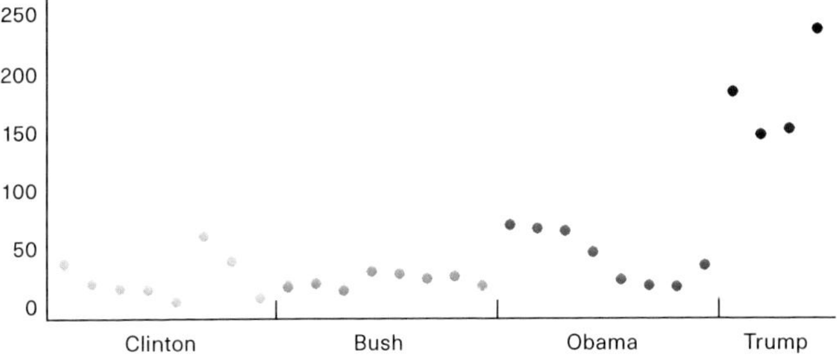

Part 2.

Point of View

This section considers how the point of view expressed in the headline demonstrates if the writer is showing certainty, doubt, or neutrality in the topic being discussed.

These points of view are based on "belief structures" used in computational approaches to natural language understanding (Ulinski, 2018). When training a computer to understand the certainty of a statement, a programmer might label text based on if the writer expresses confidence or shows uncertainty through hedging. This way, a program that is looking for factual information might put less weight on passages that express opinion or where the author is uncertain.

Direct Report

The author, journalist, or editor reports on a subject with certainty. The headline does not include the author's opinion, desires, or doubt. A simple example is "the sun will rise tomorrow."

Example Headlines

Trump Was Told Weeks Ago That Michael Flynn Withheld Truth on Russia

Published Feb. 14, 2017

Donald Trump Is Lying Again, Now About James Comey

Published May 10, 2017

Trump Repeats False Claim About El Paso Crime, This Time in El Paso

Published Feb. 12, 2019

Trump trampled decorum in the debate with cross talk, lies and mockery.

Published Sep. 30, 2020

Doubtful Report

The author, journalist, or editor reports on a subject with less certainty. The headline includes a mixed message—the claim may or may not be true, or the claim may be partially true. These headlines are inconclusive and invite readers to apply their own opinions or hopes on the topic being covered. A simple example is "it might rain tomorrow."

Example Headlines

Trump Claims 'Total Exoneration,' but Report Is Mixed on Obstruction

Published Mar. 24, 2019

Without Evidence, Trump Claims Vindication From Release of Carter Page Documents

Published Jul. 22, 2018

Looks Like the Trump Administration Lied About the Census

Published May 30, 2019

Trump Might Cheat. Activists Are Getting Ready.

Published Aug. 18, 2020

Secondhand Report

The author, journalist, or editor repeats the beliefs or statements of another person. A simple example is “the weather reporter says it will rain.”

Example Headlines

Kimmel [Calls] Trump 'a Liar' for Changing His Story on Putin Comments

Published Jul. 18, 2018

Mulvaney [Called] Trump a 'Terrible Human Being' in 2016

Published Dec. 15, 2018

Mueller [Says] Manafort Lied About Contacts With Trump Officials

Published Dec. 16, 2018

Trump [Calls] Intelligence Officials 'Naive' After They Contradict Him

Published Jan. 30, 2019

Raising Doubt

The author, journalist, or editor expresses an attitude other than belief towards a proposition, such as doubt, uncertainty, or obligation. A simple example is "will it rain tomorrow?"

These headlines often repeat the framing of the deceptive speaker and often include a question mark in their doubt. On p.12 it is shown that punctuation is often utilized to gain traction with search engines. More research could explore if there is a correlation between presenting doubt to readers and attempts to improve search engine ranking.

Example Headlines

Trump Says NATO Allies Don't Pay Their Share. Is That True?

Published May 26, 2017

Is Trump a Traitor?

Published Dec. 6, 2018

Will Trump in 2019 Be Untamed or Contained?

Published Dec. 29, 2018

Trump Accuses Saudis of Giving U.S. a Bad Deal. Is That True?

Published Apr. 28, 2019

Part 3.

Lie Types

This section discusses the mechanics of headlines and how they apply to the deceptions being covered. Previous discourse analysis research of expressions of deception in political contexts is a starting point (Galasinski, 2000). The content of headlines are grouped by categories of deception such as falsification of documents, misrepresenting context, and concealing information. The range of subject matter within these categories is contrasted with the repetition of both keywords and points of view of the headlines that cover these subjects.

External

Communication directed to other parties or audiences.

Verifiable
A statement that can be verified by historical record or scientific tests.

Non-verifiable
A statement that cannot be verified by historical record or scientific tests.

Internal

Monologue that happens with oneself or personal beliefs.

Chart on the next page is based on terms in Dariusz Galasinski's *The Language of Deception: A Discourse Analytical Study*, 1st ed., SAGE Publications, Inc, 2000.

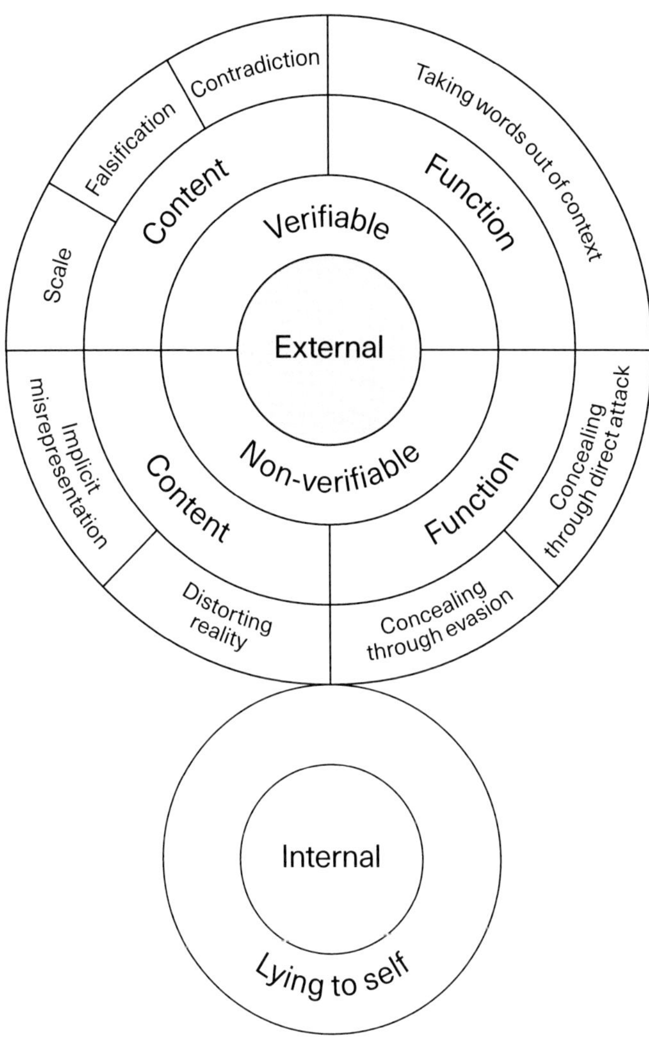
Contradiction
Falsification
Scale
Content
Verifiable
Function
Taking words out of context
External
Implicit misrepresentation
Content
Non-verifiable
Function
Concealing through direct attack
Distorting reality
Concealing through evasion
Internal
Lying to self

Distorting Scale

The speaker exaggerates, overstates, or minimizes a truth condition.

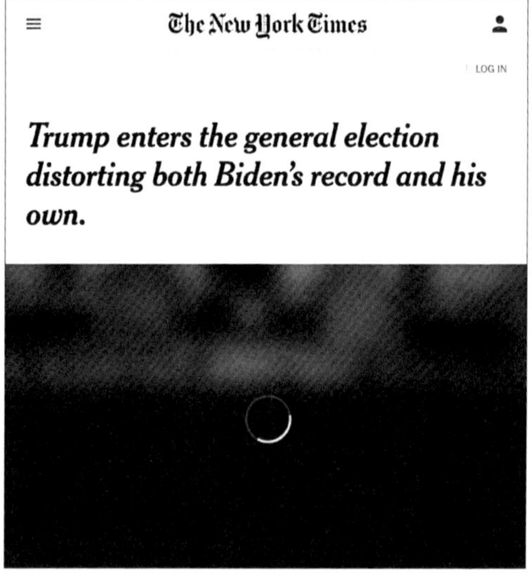
The New York Times
LOG IN

Trump enters the general election distorting both Biden's record and his own.

→ Distorting Scale

Example Headlines	Framing
Trump Exaggerates Mueller Team's Ties to Obama and Democrats Published Apr. 4, 2018	direct report
Trump Overstates Size of Tax Cuts in Speech to Farmers Published Jan. 8, 2018	direct report
Trump Exaggerates Trade Deficit With European Union by $50 Billion Published Jun. 8, 2018	direct report

Keywords

overstate, exaggerate, distort, misrepresent, minimize

Falsifying Documents

The speaker's deception involves distortion of the historical or scientific record, including fraud and the altering of documents.

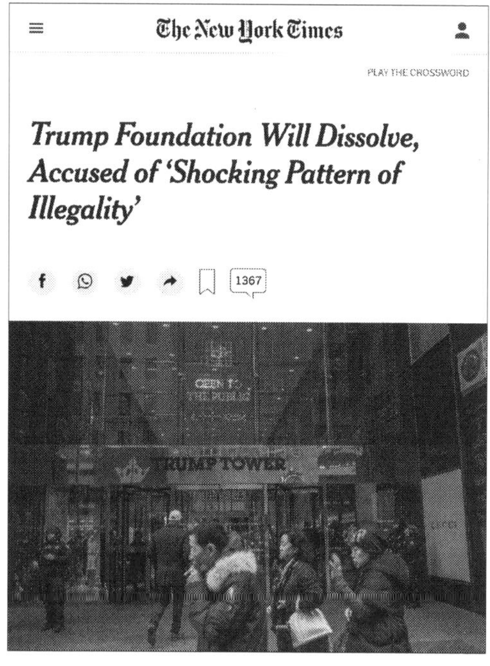
The New York Times

PLAY THE CROSSWORD

Trump Foundation Will Dissolve, Accused of 'Shocking Pattern of Illegality'

1367

Example Headlines	Framing
Trump Attacks 'Failing New York Times' Over Tax Scheme Reporting Published Oct. 3, 2018	direct report
New York Regulators Examine the Trump Family's Tax Schemes Published Oct. 4, 2018	direct report
Trump Appointees Manipulated Agency's Payday Lending Research, Ex-Staffer Claims Published Apr. 29, 2020	secondhand report

Keywords

scheme, manipulated, forged, falsify, alter

Contradiction

The speaker offers a proposition, statement, or phrase that asserts or implies both the truth and falsity of something.

Types

- **Antonym**
  Statements or words are opposite to words that describe the truth.
- **Negation**
  The truth value of one statement makes another statement invalid.
- **Numeric**
  Quantities in the statement are inaccurate.
- **Factive**
  A falsehood is presented as a fact.
- **Structure**
  False claims discuss geographic characteristics or built environments.
- **Lexical**
  Words and word order used in one statement are not compatible with words or word order from another statement.

Example Headlines

Antonym / secondhand report

Trump Says Transition's Going 'Smoothly,' Disputing Disarray Reports

Published Nov. 16, 2016

Factive / secondhand report

Trump Falsely Claims to Be First Republican to Win Wisconsin Since Eisenhower

Published Jun. 28, 2018

Negation / secondhand report

Giuliani in Public: 'It's a Fraud.' Giuliani in Court: 'This Is Not a Fraud Case.'

Published Nov. 19, 2020

Structure / secondhand report

Trump Insists He Was Right About Hurricane Dorian Heading for Alabama

Published Oct. 27, 2017

Numeric / secondhand report

Trump Falsely Claims a 10% Decrease in Illegal Border Crossings

Published May 16, 2018

Lexical / secondhand report

Trump Falsely Claims, 'I Never Said Russia Did Not Meddle'

Published Nov. 16, 2016

Taking Words out of Context

An utterance that takes on different meaning in a chosen context compared to the context when it was originally expressed.

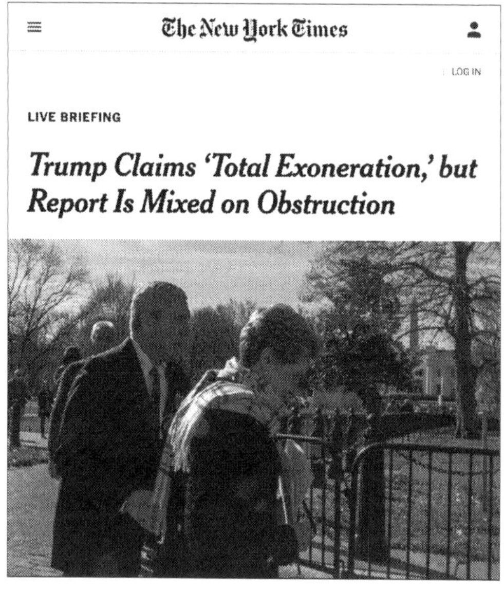
The New York Times

LOG IN

LIVE BRIEFING

Trump Claims 'Total Exoneration,' but Report Is Mixed on Obstruction

Example Headlines	Framing
Six [Claims] Trump Made at His Weekend Rally That Were [False] or [Lacked Context] Published Mar. 12, 2018	direct report
Trump Repeats [Claim] That James Clapper [']Admitted['] to Campaign Spying. It's Still [Wrong] Published May 24, 2018	secondhand report
Trump [Claims] [']Total Exoneration,['] [but] Report Is Mixed on Obstruction Published Mar. 24, 2019	doubtful report
Trump Spread Multiple [Conspiracy Theories] on Monday. Here Are Their [Roots] Published Sep. 1, 2020	direct report

Distorting Reality

The speaker's statements require different background conditions to exist in order to be true.

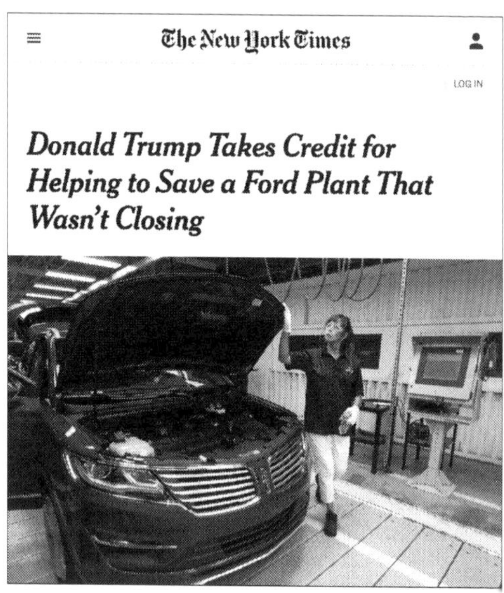

The New York Times

LOG IN

Donald Trump Takes Credit for Helping to Save a Ford Plant That Wasn't Closing

Example Headlines	Framing
Donald Trump Takes Credit for Helping to Save a Ford Plant [That Wasn't] Closing Published Nov. 18, 2016	direct report
Trump Has a Habit of Quoting His Allies on Twitter Saying Things They [Never Said] Published Dec. 20, 2019	direct report
Trump [Sows Doubt] on Voting. It Keeps Some People Up at Night Published May 24, 2020	direct report

Keywords

sows doubt, that wasn't, never said

Evasion

The speaker pretends to give a cooperative answer by either changing the context of the question and/or focus of questioning.

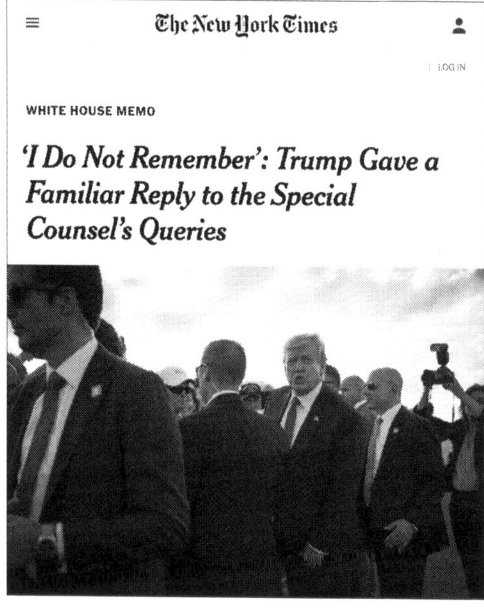

The New York Times

LOG IN

WHITE HOUSE MEMO

'I Do Not Remember': Trump Gave a Familiar Reply to the Special Counsel's Queries

Example Headlines	Framing
Donald Trump Jr.'s Two Different Explanations for Russian Meeting Published Jul. 10, 2017	secondhand report
Trump Discloses Cohen Payment, Raising Questions About Previous Omission Published May 16, 2018	doubtful report
'I Do Not Remember': Trump Gave a Familiar Reply to the Special Counsel's Queries Published Apr. 20, 2019	secondhand report

Keywords

sidestep, omission, mislead, evade, conceal, play down, downplay

Direct Attack

The speaker manipulates the framing of an argument through attacking another speaker or entity.

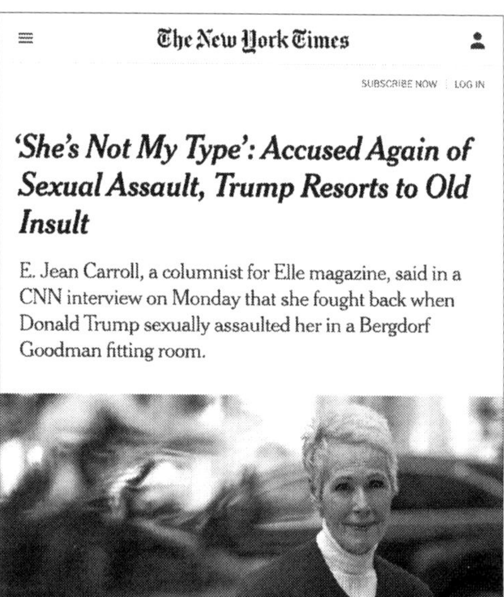

The New York Times

SUBSCRIBE NOW | LOG IN

'She's Not My Type': Accused Again of Sexual Assault, Trump Resorts to Old Insult

E. Jean Carroll, a columnist for Elle magazine, said in a CNN interview on Monday that she fought back when Donald Trump sexually assaulted her in a Bergdorf Goodman fitting room.

Example Headlines	Framing
Donald Trump [Dismisses] Latest Accuser: 'Oh, I'm Sure She's Never Been Grabbed Before' Published Oct. 24, 2016	secondhand report
As Melania Trump Faces Plagiarism Claims, Her Staff [Lashes Out] at News Media Published May 8, 2018	direct report
After [dismissing] an investigation into his taxes as 'fake news,' Trump [lashes out] at the suggestion that he is not as wealthy as he claims Published Sep. 28, 2020	secondhand report

Keywords

lash out, dismiss, insult

Lying to Self

The speaker has a motivated false belief. This includes a process of denying or mischaracterizing evidence that opposes one's belief.

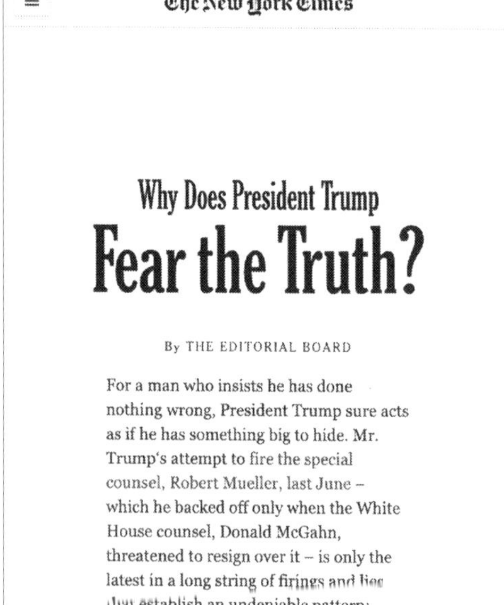

The New York Times

Why Does President Trump

Fear the Truth?

By THE EDITORIAL BOARD

For a man who insists he has done nothing wrong, President Trump sure acts as if he has something big to hide. Mr. Trump's attempt to fire the special counsel, Robert Mueller, last June – which he backed off only when the White House counsel, Donald McGahn, threatened to resign over it – is only the latest in a long string of firings and lies that establish an undeniable pattern:

Example Headlines	**Framing**
Press Secretary Affirms that Trump [Believes Lie] of Millions of Illegal Voters Published Jan. 24, 2017	secondhand report
Can Donald Trump [Handle the Truth?] Published Jan. 28, 2017	raising doubt
Why Trump Still [Believes] [(Wrongly)] That Ukraine Hacked the D.N.C. Published Nov. 26, 2019	direct report

Keywords

believes lie, believes himself

Manipulated Images and Videos

Speaker shares photos or videos that provide evidence for, or suggest a falsehood. Examples include manipulated videos and audio.

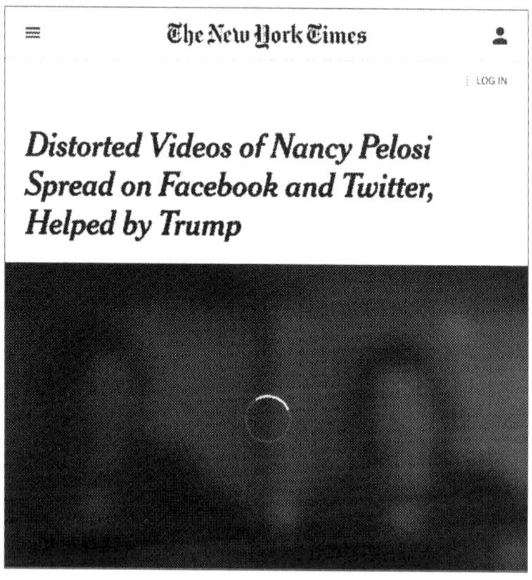
The New York Times

LOG IN

Distorted Videos of Nancy Pelosi Spread on Facebook and Twitter, Helped by Trump

Example Headlines	**Framing**
Distorted Videos of Nancy Pelosi Spread on Facebook and Twitter, Helped by Trump Published May 24, 2019	direct report
After Biden plays 'Despacito' at an event, Trump shares a doctored video replacing it with an anti-police song Published Sep. 15, 2020	direct report
Trump Shares Two Doctored Videos of Biden Published Sep. 16, 2020	direct report

Keywords

doctored, distorted

Part 4.

Conclusion

The world watched in shock and disbelief as Donald Trump and his closest followers contested the 2020 U.S. election results. What followed was an armed insurrection against the Capitol, threatening lawmakers and our democracy.

Thirteen days after this horrific event, *The New York Times* topped off their incessant coverage of Trump (almost 2,000 headlines on the front page in four years[1]) with a montage of these headlines. To promote this story, the *Times* tweeted (see next page) an image of their front page headline from the previous election, "Trump Triumphs." So, less than two weeks after Trump and a large number of his supporters refused to accept the election results, the *Times* was reminding their Twitter followers that he won.

That's the worry. In assembling the data in this book, am I also amplifying the lies—the outliars—that I'm so interested in analyzing? For me, filtering thousands of headlines, thousands of deceptions, through the sieve of Excel tables and Python scripts has allowed me to reckon with this material. Processing this historical moment as data has been my attempt to heal from a period that's left me shaken.

My background is in computational approaches to natural language understanding. Simply put, I write code that instructs computers to find patterns in human language. The goal is to make programs that decipher what a text is about. I analyzed these headlines like I would a machine learning challenge, one where I would be training

1. https://twitter.com/nytimes/status/1351586495749099520

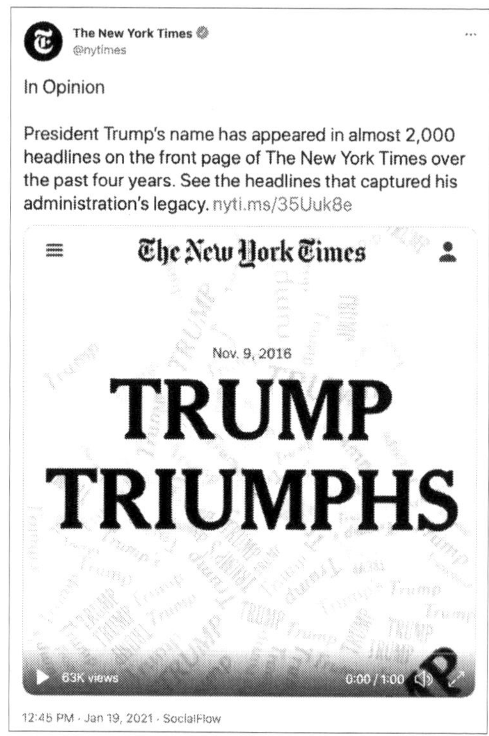

Tweet posted by *The New York Times* thirteen days after the Capitol attack.

an algorithm to detect if the author of a headline was certain in their statement, and if the headline was discussing a deceptive act. Normally these techniques would be applied to social media posts, not constricted to the domain of *The New York Times's* headlines.

In the end, I didn't make a new lie detector.

What I actually found was there's no natural language recipe for determining truth. If there were, our online discourse would be easier to manage. Human language can be expressed and composed in infinite ways—context is also needed to decipher meaning. Almost every other headline in this book would be an outlier for an automated classifier.

This book provides the vantage point of scale. Interpreting these headlines as textual data can serve as a valuable artifact of this time. While we can continue to hope that the news media will learn from their mistakes, we as readers can be empowered. Being aware of these patterns in deception and headline framing allows us to receive this media differently. We can apply this analytical lens to mentally filter out stories that are unimportant, and be more aware of how deceptive narratives are spread. In this way, the title "Outliars" is asking journalists and news organizations to call out lies directly. In other cases, it is better to leave the liar out of coverage altogether.

Angie Waller, 2021

References

Bulik, Mark. "Which Headlines Attract Most Readers?" *The New York Times*, June 13, 2016. https://www.nytimes.com/2016/06/13/insider/which-headlines-attract-most-readers.html, accessed Feb. 15, 2021.

Christin, Angèle. *Metrics at Work: Journalism and the Contested Meaning of Algorithms.* Princeton University Press, 2020.

Galasinski, Dariusz. *The Language of Deception: A Discourse Analytical Study,* 1st ed., SAGE Publications, Inc, 2000.

Jiang, Shan, et al. "Who's the Guinea Pig?" *Proceedings of the Conference on Fairness, Accountability, and Transparency*, 2019.

The New York Times Company, *2020 Annual Report,* 2020. https://nytco-assets.nytimes.com/2021/03/Final-NYT-2020-Annual-Report.pdf, accessed Apr. 15,2021.

Ritter, Alan, et al. "It's a Contradiction -- No, it's Not: A Case Study using Functional Relations." *Proceedings of the 2008 Conference on Empirical Methods in Natural Language Processing*, 2008.

Ulinski, Morgan, et al. "Using Hedge Detection to Improve Committed Belief Tagging." *Proceedings of the Workshop on Computational Semantics beyond Events and Roles*, 2018.

Data provided by *The New York Times*, https://developer.nytimes.com.

Source code and data for this project are available at https://github.com/angiewaller/outliars-not-outliers.

Credits

Design by Anisa Suthayalai. Special thanks to Emily Saltz, Patrick Davison, and William Jordan for support and guidance.

Works that touch on these themes and informed this book include:

Angèle Christin's book *Metrics at Work* compares how a newsroom in France and one in the U.S. responded to the age of digital analytics. She shows how dashboard tools that measure clicks and shares used by newsrooms have a wide range of interpretations depending on the culture and goals of the news outlet.

Oxygen of Amplification by Whitney Phillips guides journalists in strategies that can stop the spread of misinformation. She shows how the media is gamed and manipulated by malicious actors and the harms that result when journalists repeat their framings.

Lexicon of Lies by Caroline Jack is a report that lays out the terms that are used to define problematic content and misinformation. By laying out these terms, her report shows how different kinds of problematic content are spread and how they are received. She proposes that understanding the limitations of these concepts can help better intervention strategies.

Source Hacking by Joan Donovan and Brian Friedberg details how techniques used by media manipulators target journalists during breaking news events to pick up falsehoods and unknowingly amplify them to the public.

George Lakoff's work, particularly *Don't Think of an Elephant,* explains how responding to an opponent's framing of an argument is only buttressing their perspective (or lie), sealing it into the public's consciousness.

@j_e_d has a Twitter bot called *Editing TheGrayLady* (@nyt_diff) that publishes the before and afters of *New York Times's* headlines and abstracts so you can see their editorial decisions in real time.

Surya Mattu's Twitter bot, @postpoetics, shows hilarious groupings of headlines that were tested on *New York Post* headlines. Lenticular prints of these tests are available at unknownunknowns.org.

Outliars

Published by
Unknown Unknowns
New York, NY
USA

ISBN 978-0-9913923-5-3

UNKNOWN UNKNOWNS
unknownunknowns.org